WAKE UP THE
SLEEPING
GIANTS

Dorothy McDaniel

WESTBOW
PRESS
A DIVISION OF THOMAS NELSON
& ZONDERVAN

WestBow Press books may be ordered through booksellers or by contacting:

WestBow Press
A Division of Thomas Nelson & Zondervan
1663 Liberty Drive
Bloomington, IN 47403
www.westbowpress.com
1 (866) 928-1240

ISBN: 978-1-4908-2776-6 (sc)
ISBN: 978-1-4908-2778-0 (e)

Library of Congress Control Number: 2014903576

Printed in the United States of America.

WestBow Press rev. date: 04/17/2014

CONTENTS

IN DEDICATION

I dedicate this book in memory of my late husband William "Earl" McDaniel, Sr. and my beloved Mother Victoria P. Whittaker.

I praise God and give love to all of my children, grandchildren and great-grandchildren.

To my sisters and brother who are yoke fellows in the Gospel of Jesus Christ.

To my other family members as well.

ACKNOWLEDGEMENTS

I am indeed grateful for my Intercessory Prayer Partners, who pray with me and for me on a regular basis, and for others who support the ministry as well.

I give special thanks to Minister Janice King for the personal and dedicated service she graciously provided to assist me with publishing this book. May God's blessings and favor always abound in your life.

Special gratitude to Mrs. Shirley Jackson for her prayers and generous support to Miracles of Faith Ministries, Inc.

Special thanks to Mrs. Shau-Ann King for all the assistance she gave to making this book a reality. "Thank you."

Most of all I thank my Lord and Saviour, Jesus The Christ for all He's doing in my life.

FOREWORD

Wake up the Sleeping Giants

I was inspired to write this book, after meeting the Reverend Dr. Moses Okpara, an African Missionary from Nigeria, West Africa. He was the president of Bible Way Ministries, a missionary ministry in Africa. This was Dr. Okpara's third visit to Wayne County, North Carolina. Dr. Okpara stated God told him that someday he would go to the United States of America somewhere and preach "Wake up the Sleeping Giants!" During a newspaper interview, the reporter had asked Dr. Okpara, why he chose to visit Wayne County and he responded that he couldn't really understand it, only he had a burden for Wayne County. He also believed that God had sent him to America to wake up the sleeping giants. Dr. Okpara came to Helping Hands Mission and met with Pastor Lula Newkirk and me requesting assistance in having a prayer crusade in Mount Olive, North Carolina

We agreed to assist him with his prayer crusade. We was confident that the prayer crusade would be a success. The crusade was scheduled to take place on August 19 1999 at Mt Olive College, Rogers Chapel. The purpose of this crusade was to bring believers together to pray that the walls of division, racism, and segregation be pulled down within the body of Christ, especially among pastors.

Dr. Okpara was adamant about the crusade. During our meeting he made a profound statement that "Whatever God begins He completes and if God's prophet dies someone else will take over." On August 19, 1999 my prayer partners and I, along with others went to Mt Olive College, excited about the crusade.

Imagine my shock when I was told that Dr. Okpara died mysteriously on August 18, 1999, the day before the crusade was to begin (this meant the mission was aborted). Now fifteen years later, as I reflect on Dr. Okpara's mission and demise, I am reminded of Moses' death. When God told Joshua, "Moses my servant is dead, now therefore arise, go over this Jordan, thou and all the people (Joshua 1:2)."

Upon meditating on that Word, I gasped in surprise realizing that Dr. Okpara's name was "Moses" as well - Dr. Moses Okpara. I thought once again of the statement he made at the last meeting we had in 1999. When God's prophet dies, someone else will take over.

The Holy Spirit prompted me to hurry and complete the manuscript that I had already started, "Wake up the sleeping giants."

INTRODUCTION

Sleep is defined as a naturally recurring state of being, which causes an absence, or reduction of consciousness and sensory stimuli; by relaxing voluntary muscles. Sleep is essential for maintaining a healthy body, physically and mentally. Sleep enhances the function of the body's immune, skeletal, nervous, and the muscular system as well. (*From Wikipedia, the free encyclopedia*)

In the Bible, sleep is often used to describe death. When Lazarus died, Jesus said: "Our friend Lazarus sleepeth; but I go that I may awake him out of sleep (John 11:11)."

His disciples said, "Lord if he sleeps, he shall do well!" Then said Jesus unto them plainly: "Lazarus is dead (John 11:14)." Lazarus was awakened out of his slumber at the profound command of Jesus to come forth. Lazarus responded to the command of God and came forth while yet being bound. Jesus spoke specifically to Lazarus, calling him by name. Knowing the power of God, some theologians surmise that if Jesus had spoken in general, everyone who was asleep would have come forth as well. What a mighty God!

During the natural sleep, some people are not easily awakened. Therefore, they rely on alarm clocks or other devices. The same can be said of being spiritually dormant or asleep. Likewise, the same can be said of those who need a spiritual awakening.

God is sounding an alarm for his people to be awakened out of their spiritual sleep, because they have slept long enough. God is speaking emphatically through his Holy Word and prophets, saying "Blow ye the trumpet in Zion and sound an alarm in my Holy Mountain; let all the inhabitants of the land tremble; for the day of the Lord cometh for it is nigh at hand (Joel 2:1)."

The alarm has sounded; the God of the universe has spoken. This is not the time to press the snooze button or turn over spiritually, nor remain in a state of slumber because we are engaged in a spiritual war against the ruler of darkness.

Some Christians are resting comfortably and do not want to be drawn out of their comfort zone. Some will even get disgruntled or perturbed when their sleep status is interrupted. The question is "How long will thou sleep O sluggard? When will thou arise out of thy sleep? (Proverbs 6:9)."

While some natural sleep is essential for the well-being of humans, spiritual sleep and slumber is totally unacceptable to God. "But while men slept his enemy came and sowed tares among the wheat and went his way (Matthew 13:25)."

The body of Christ was asleep spiritually when Madam O'Hara, persevered and took public prayer out of schools. Spiritual lights of many devout men and women of God have been diminished due to their deviant life styles, and worldly pleasures. Some were once on fire for God, but eventually became weary in well doing, thus, drifted away and became lukewarm.

Others are just spiritually lazy. After having resisted the prompting and prodding of the Holy Ghost, many have resorted to spending quality time on Facebook, Twitter, and other modern technologies, thus fallen asleep spiritually.

People often take time for granted, with the idea that they have plenty of time to procrastinate, and yet do what is required of them. They fail to realize that time waits for no man. Solomon said "to everything there is a season and a time to every purpose under the heaven (Ecclesiastes 3:1)." Therefore, we must redeem the time, realizing God has given us enough time to do his will.

Physical Giants

Physical giants are defined as human beings of an abnormally large size and endowed with super human strength, having the capabilities to do mighty physical exploits. (*From Wikipedia, the free encyclopedia*)

Goliath was a prime example of a physical giant, who trusted in his own strength, and boasted of his mighty physical power, dressed in super heavy armor, wielding a super-sized sword and shield.

Spiritual Giants

Spiritual giants on the other hand are born again believers, who are filled with the Holy Spirit of God. Their strength is not contingent upon their physical size or stature. They are dressed entirely from head to toe in the whole armor of God, which is invisible to the naked eye.

This armor consists of their loins being girt about with truth. They wear the breastplate of righteousness, their feet shod with the gospel of peace, their faith is their shield, salvation is their helmet, and the Word of God is their sword.

The spiritual giants' weapons are not carnal but mighty, through God to the pulling down of strongholds. Therefore, spiritual giants are much stronger than physical giants. Spiritual giants are fully armed and are extremely dangerous, wielding weapons consisting of short and long-range missiles that can cause mass destruction to the kingdom of darkness. This is the main reason why the devil wants the people of God to remain in a passive state or slumber mode, because of the destruction that will be wrought against his kingdom.

The Bible says the whole creation itself is groaning, awaiting the manifestation of the people of God to take back the control of the earth from the devil. This is definitely not a time to be asleep spiritually because we are engaged in warfare, and God's people are on the front line.

We are not fighting against flesh and blood, but against principalities, and the evil forces of this world. When the people of God are passive, the kingdom of darkness accelerates at an alarming rate.

The state of passivity is not due to a lack of hearing God's Word, because the Word of God is being preached, and published throughout the world in various ways. The problem is due to a lack of obedience to the Word of God. We have been commissioned and empowered by the Spirit of God to do greater works. Jesus said, "Verily, verily I say unto you, he that believeth on me, the work that I do shall he do also, and greater works then these shall he do because I go unto my father (John 14:12)."

CHAPTER I

AWAKENED TO LIFE

God Created Man

It all began in the Garden of Eden, after God created the whole world, with everything therein, including all plant and animal life; He was pleased with His creation. God needed someone to care for the beautiful garden He had made, and to have someone on earth to communicate with, and express His love. So, God said, "Let us make man in our image, after our likeness; and let them have dominion over the fish of the sea, and over the fowls of the air, and over the cattle, and over all the earth.... (Genesis 1:26)." God executed his plan, and created the man Adam, whom, "the Lord God formed of the dust of the ground and breathed into his nostrils the breath of life, and man became a living soul (Genesis 2:7)."

Therefore, God put Adam in the Garden of Eden to care for, and take charge of it. God delegated to Adam the awesome responsibility to name every living creature He had created. All the animals that God created had mates, but Adam had no companion. God being a loving caring God, said, "It is not good that the man should be alone; I will make him a helpmeet for him (Genesis 2:18)."

God Created Woman

God performed the first supernatural surgical procedure by His Holy Power; administered Holy anesthesia, induced Adam into a deep sleep, extracted a rib from his side, and closed up his flesh miraculously. Then God performed another miracle in the Garden of Eden. He sculptured the rib that He removed from Adam's side, and made, "Woman" a special helpmeet for him. I envisioned, God, taking this newly created, beautiful woman by her arm and escorted her across the beautiful lawn of the Garden of Eden. The woman's hair flowing in the wind. The birds chirping excitedly, the other animals staring in sheer amazement as God strolled across the exotic Garden of Eden, walking past the beautiful shrubbery and flowers which depicted all colors of the spectrum, in route to present her to Adam, her husband.

Adam, no doubt being completely captivated by this beautiful creature that only God from heaven could create, praised God as he embraced his bride. She was the prettiest woman in the whole wide world. Adam had the privilege of naming his bride; he called her Eve, because she was to be the mother of all living creatures.

Remember now, Adam and Eve were the perfect innocent couple. They lived in a perfect environment, in the presence of a perfect Holy God. Life was good. They were in daily fellowship with God, and they had dominion over everything in the garden. God given authority always requires obedience, responsibility, and accountability.

God commanded Adam, saying "of every tree of the garden thou mayeth freely eat, but of the tree of the knowledge of good and evil, thou shalt not eat of it, for on the day that thou eatest thereof thou shalt surely die (Genesis 2:16-17)."

CHAPTER II

AWAKENED TO SIN

The process of sin began when Eve began to spend time in conversation with the serpent in the Garden of Eden. This was a great mistake because the serpent was the shrewdest and craftiest of all the other creatures in the garden. The serpent took advantage of Eve's innocence and began to question the command God had given them regarding the forbidden tree. Eve repeated to the serpent what God had said, "you shalt not eat of it, neither shalt you touch it, lest you die (Genesis 3:3)."

The serpent rebuked God's command saying, "You shall not surely die" calling God a liar! He continued to convince and deceive Eve telling her that if she ate from that tree, her eyes would be open and that she would be wise just like God.

I imagine that the serpent captivated Eve's interest, telling her all sorts of lies no doubt about the benefits she would get from simply eating the fruit. He probably used alluring language, making the fruit appear tempting for the first time. Perhaps, the serpent's power of persuasion overwhelmed Eve to the point that her lust for the fruit caused her to disobey God's command. As we know, Eve took of the forbidden fruit, and ate it. At that moment, the first phase of sin was conceived.

have often wondered why the serpent chose to approach Eve, rather than Adam. This determination was not addressed in the book of Genesis during the fall. As I mused upon this thought, I received the revelation that the serpent did not approach Adam first because, Adam being a male did not have a womb. He did not have the ability to conceive Satan's spiritual corrupted seed, nor give birth to the seed.

On the other hand, the serpent being more subtle than all the other beast God created, knew that the natural entry into the earth's realm is through a woman. So in order to execute his wicked plan, he had to plant a spiritually corrupted sin seed into the virgin womb of Eve's heart. This was done so that she may conceive "sin" and that sin be birthed into the souls of all humanity, because Eve was the mother of all humanity. At the very moment Eve committed the act of disobeying God's Word, the nature of sin was conceived. When these events transpired, Adam must have been asleep or walking in other parts of the garden.

I believe that Eve's world as she once knew it was turned upside down after the birth of sin. Not only did she have knowledge of good and evil, but she was able to experience emotions generated by sin. Namely the overwhelming sense of guilt, gross shame, fear, anger, condemnation and every other evil emotion caused by sin.

Pride entered her heart when she became aware of her physical attributes. Her thought process was enlightened to the ways of the world. Eve now had an edge over Adam because she was wise in ways he was not, because he had not yet eaten the forbidden fruit.

No doubt, after Eve realized what a horrific deed she had done she was compelled to get Adam involved in the process for she was not going to bear the blame alone. Only God knows how she executed her scheme, but I believe that Eve used her newly discovered femininity and sensuality to charm Adam to eat the forbidden fruit.

Remember Adam was still in the state of innocence and Eve was already enlightened. I believe Eve wooed and coerced Adam so much so, that he found her feminine power of persuasion totally irresistible; thus, he took of the fruit from Eve's hands and ate it. The Bible says "And the eyes of them both were opened (Genesis 3:7)." Afterwards, they tried to hide themselves from God. It is no wonder that Adam told God, "The woman whom thou gavest to be with me; she gave me of the tree, and I did eat (Genesis 3:11)."

Adam had fallen prey to Eve's deceptive and seductive spell and was taken down by eating the forbidden fruit. Thus, Satan's deceptive plan for the fall of humanity was complete. From the beginning of time, women have used an age-old trick to cause men to have a downfall. Men and Women are still falling under the seductive spirit of Satan by partaking of forbidden fruits.

CHAPTER III

AWAKENED UNTO SALVATION

God was not surprised by the fall of man because He is God. Thus being a just God, he gave them the right to make choices, but gave them the consequences of their choices as well. They chose the wrong path. God had an alternate plan to be executed in the fullness of time.

> "Wherefore as by one man sin entered into the world, and death by sin; and so death passed upon all men, for that all have sinned (Romans 5:12)."

> "For the wages of sin is death; but the gift of God is eternal life through Jesus Christ our Lord (Romans 6:23)."

> The Word also says, "For as by one man's disobedience many were made sinners so by the obedience of one shall many be made righteous (Romans 5:19)."

> "But God commended His love toward us, in that, while we were yet sinners, Christ died for us. Much more then, being now justified by his blood, we shall be saved from wrath through Him (Romans 5:8, 9)."

The plan of salvation was set in motion when God's Word became flesh and a woman was chosen, the Virgin Mary to be impregnated by the Holy Spirit. She would be the legitimate vessel to bring His Holy Son, Jesus, into the earth's realm to destroy the work of Satan and to redeem a lost humanity.

Jesus, the Son of God, humbled Himself and became obedient to the will of God, He was scourged and brutally beaten beyond recognition before He was hung on the rugged cross. He was sinless, but He took on Himself the sins of the world. He became sin for us that we might become the righteousness of God through Him. He was the sacrificial lamb that was slain for the atonement of our sins. As He was dying, Jesus said, "It is finished" Our sin debt was paid in full.

Jesus, our Lord and Savior, was buried. But as we know it that's not the end of the story. He arose from the dead with all power in heaven and on earth. Those who accept his finished work, it is as if they had never sinned. They are justified. Before his ascension to heaven, he commissioned his disciples to "go ye into all the world, and preach the gospel to every creature" (Mark 16:15)."

"And these signs shall follow them that believe; in my name shall they cast out devils; they shall speak with new tongues; they shall take up serpents; and if they drink any deadly thing, it shall not hurt them; they shall lay hands on the sick; and they shall recover (Mark 16:17–18)."

Jesus is still speaking to his disciples. The Spiritual Giants must be awakened in order to be able to execute this great command.

There are many Christians who have a form of godliness, but are denying the power thereof (2 Timothy 3:5).

The Word of God is being greatly published throughout the earth, but there will be a greater demonstration of the power of God because Jesus said so. Paul wrote, "And my speech and my preaching was not with enticing words of man's wisdom; but in demonstration of the spirit and of power; that your faith should not stand in the wisdom of men, but in the power of God (1 Corinthians 2:4-5)."

CHAPTER IV

ASLEEP AT THE WRONG TIME

There are numerous accounts of spiritual giants who slept at the most inopportune time. An example of this would be, Jesus on the night He was betrayed in the garden of Gethsemane with Peter, James, and John. Jesus who was heavily burdened due to His pending crucifixion, said to His disciples, "My soul is exceedingly sorrowful unto death, tarry ye here, and watch (Mark 14:34)." Jesus prayed fervently to His Father, that the bitter cup that He had to bear be taken away. That if there was any other way that salvation could be brought to humanity let it be done. Jesus knew that all things were possible with God, but He also knew what the will of God was, so He prayed that God's will be done. Jesus arose from prayer and went to His disciples and found them fast asleep. Jesus addressed Peter: "Simon, sleepest thou? Could not thou watch one hour? Watch ye and pray, lest you enter into temptation, the spirit truly is ready, but the flesh is weak (Mark 14:37, 38)."

I believe Jesus called Peter by name because of a conversation He had earlier that evening when He told them that they would be offended that the Shepherd would be smitten and the sheep scattered. Peter was the only one who spoke out with the utmost confidence and conviction saying "Although all shall be offended, yet will not I (Mark 14:29)."

9

Jesus knowing all things, told Peter he would deny Him three times on that same night letting Peter know that he was not as strong as he thought he was. Peter insisted, "If I should die with thee I will not deny thee in any wise. Likewise also said they all (Mark 14:31)."

Jesus left them again and prayed the same prayer to His father, returned again to His disciples and found them still asleep. Jesus left them a third time, continuing to pray fervently to God saying the same thing. The Bible says in the fourteenth chapter of Mark that Jesus was in such agony that His sweat became as drops of blood, falling on the ground.

Jesus was all alone; his disciples who had vowed that they were willing to die with him, especially Peter were sound asleep. They were totally oblivious to the intense suffering that Jesus was experiencing. They went to sleep when Jesus needed their support the most.

After Jesus finished praying, He had resolved in His spirit that God's Will had to be done and He accepted that He was going to be crucified and went back to where He found His disciples asleep the third time and said: "Sleep on now, and take your rest; it is enough (Mark 14:41)." Jesus knew *His* purpose for being on planet earth, and He knew He and He alone had to fulfill His mission. He was the Lamb of God, to be sacrificed on the rugged cross, for the salvation of all humanity.

Asleep at the Wrong Place

The book of Judges, sixteenth chapter, gives an account of Sampson, a Nazarite and a spiritual giant, who was fast asleep in Delilah's lap when his anointing walked. Sampson was raised up by God to deliver the Israelites from the oppression of the Philistines.

When God gets ready to change course and deliver lost and suffering humanity or save a generation He does the following. He has a baby born somewhere and when that child is old enough, He puts a call upon their life by which He empowers them to accomplish His purpose. God gives a sign or a point of contact to help release their faith. For example, God gave Moses a rod in his hand to demonstrate the power of God by which he was able to deliver God's people. Elijah had a mantle in his hand. The baby Jesus was wrapped in swaddling clothes, lying in a manger; this was the sign for the shepherds to know who He was. John the Baptist saw the Holy Spirit descend upon Jesus's head in the form of a dove, as God had told him that this would be the sign that Jesus was His Son. The sign in Sampson's life was his long hair.

Sampson's mother was barren and an Angel appeared unto her and announced that she was going to conceive a son. Along with the announcement, she was given instructions of things she could not eat or drink during her pregnancy. Not only that, but she was told that this child would be born a Nazarite unto God. That no razor should come upon his head. His hair was never to be cut because he was a chosen vessel to be used by God.

As a young man, the Spirit of God began to move upon Sampson and made his arms as strong as steel. The Spirit did not dwell within Sampson, but moved upon him and empowered him to do supernatural things. One day a lion attacked him and he tore the lion apart with his bare hands. On another occasion, Sampson went to the city of his enemy "Gaza" and fell asleep. The Philistines found out he was there, locked the gates of the city, and planned to kill Sampson that next day. At midnight, Sampson woke up and found that he was locked inside. He walked out to the gate, and the Spirit of God came upon him, strengthening him to rip the gate from the hinges. Then he threw it upon his shoulders and walked away, carrying the gate up a hill and left it as a trophy.

Sampson would avenge the Israelites when the Philistines attacked and robbed them. But Sampson had a weakness, and that weakness was the appeal of beautiful women who were not of the Jewish race. This weakness caused Sampson to rebel against God's plan for his life. The devil began to creep in as Sampson began to backslide in being faithful to God. Sampson fell in love with Delilah. He decided he would make a conquest of her, while Delilah had a plan of a conquest for her own self.

Delilah began to use her sexuality to allure him in order to discover the secret of his great power. She used lust and passion to get Sampson's mind off God and to reduce his faith to the level of her lust. Perhaps she knew if she could divide his thinking and believing in God, he would be like any other man. Unfortunately, Sampson thought he could handle the situation as Delilah began her subtle campaign to discover the sign of God in his life, which was the secret of his strength.

Sampson foolishly decided to play along with her because he felt he could stop when he wanted too. As the saying says, "If you play with fire you are most likely to get burned." Solomon says, "Can a man take fire in his bosom and his clothes not be burned? (Proverbs 6:27)." Sampson's life was liken to a speeding train on a track. It's hard to come to an abrupt stop.

Delilah insisted upon knowing the secret of his strength. He told her on one occasion if she would bind him with seven green withes, she would discover his strength, which she did, and he broke them off his arms like twine. Again, he suggested that if he was bound with new rope, even they were no match for his strength. All of her prior efforts were futile. But Delilah did not give up as she was very cunning and persistent.

Then, Sampson suggested weaving his hair. Delilah was now getting closer to the truth when she saw he had mocked her three times, she went into a rage and demanded that he leave. Delilah did not do this until she had filled his mind with lust for her body.

Sampson returned to his people, but could not stay. He had begun to doze spiritually. He was very lethargic, because Delilah had left her mark upon his soul. He tried to get her out of his mind but he had gone too far. His faith in God had dwindled. He did nothing to break off the relationship with the woman the devil had sent to destroy him and abort the work of God. His lust for her took control of him; and he was snarled in the fowlers trap.

The cause for which he was born began to fade. He no longer responded to the cries and desperate need of the people. The Philistines actions did not appall him anymore. All he could think of was Delilah. The giant was drifting into a deep sleep. So Sampson returned to her. "He goeth after her straightway, as an ox goeth to the slaughter, or as a fool to the correction of the stocks: Till a dart strike through his liver; as a bird hasteth to the snare, and knoweth not that it is for his life; her house is the way to Hell, going down to the chambers of death (Proverbs 7:22, 23, 27)." Delilah had won.

Sampson, trusted her and revealed to her the secret of his strength. This giant of a man than laid his head in Delilah's lap and went to sleep. While he slept with the enemy of his soul, she had all of his hair cut off, and he was stripped of the Power of God because he could not hold out any longer. "With her much fair speech she caused him to yield, with the flattering of her lips she forced him (Proverbs 7:21)."

In the morning Delilah shook the sleeping giant and woke him up saying, "Sampson the Philistines are upon thee." Sampson jumped up, flexed his muscles, and said, "I will go out as at other times before, and shake myself (Judges 16:20)." Little did he know that the power of the Lord had departed from him and he was void of strength. God was gone. Strength was gone. And then, he discovered his hair was gone as well.

While this Spiritual giant slept, his anointing walked and God's purpose delayed by the enemy's tactic. The Philistines gouged out Sampson's eyes and sent him to prison in total defeat. He was used as a mule at a grinding mill. As time passed, and he carried out his gruesome duties, his hair began to grow back. Sampson's enemies were oblivious to the regrowth of his hair. With his regrowth, came the restoration of his physical strength, which gave Sampson renewed hope that God's purpose for his life would be fulfilled.

Shortly after his hair grew back, the Philistines prepared a feast to celebrate their idol god Dagon. They sent for Sampson to entertain the guests that were there. When Sampson was brought into the temple, they sent a boy out to lead him around to parade in front of the guests. As they shouted and jeered, Sampson had the boy to take him over to stand between the two main pillars which supported the roof of the temple, placed his arms around the pillar of the temple and raised his sightless eyes toward heaven and prayed to God Almighty. "O Lord God, remember me, I pray thee and strengthen me I pray thee only this once, O' God that I may be at once avenged of the Philistines for my two eyes (Judges 16:28)." And Sampson said, "Let me die with the Philistines (Judges 16:30)."

Sampson sent the boy away. He then bowed himself and the spirit of God empowered him again, allowing him to pull the building down, destroying all that was present, including himself. The number of Philistines he killed at his death was more than he killed in his life.

Sampson an awesome Spiritual giant that slept at the wrong time in the wrong place. But, he was still able to fulfill the will of God.

CHAPTER V

SPIRITUALLY ASLEEP

Many prayer warriors were spiritually asleep when an Atheist had prayer banned in the public school system. Since then, there has been an acceleration of moral decay, bullying and horrific murders as a result of prayerlessness in the schools.

After the ban it became obvious that saints needed to pray even more. Thank God that prayer cannot be banned from the hearts, minds, and mouths of Christians.

We as members of the body of Christ should ban together to provide prayer coverage for our homes, communities, local, and national leaders as well. This is even more important as we see the impending signs of the time of Christ's return.

We have to stand on the Word of God with full assurance that He will do just what He said, "If my people which are called by my name, shall humble themselves and pray, and seek my face, and turn from their wicked ways, then will I hear from heaven, and will forgive their sin, and will heal their land (2 Chronicles 7:14)."

The Sleeping Prophet

Jonah was a prophet of God who chose to blatantly disobey God's command. God commanded him to go to Nineveh and cry out against their wickedness. Jonah chose to go his own way and do his own thing. He boarded a ship going in the opposite direction, curled up and went fast asleep. His actions proved detrimental to himself and the ship crew as well.

Jonah thought he was running from the presence of God. He should have read the Word of God, which says;

> "Whither shall I go from thy Spirit? Or whither shall I flee from thy presence" if I ascend up into heaven thou art there; if I make my bed in hell, behold thou art there; if I take the wings of the morning and dwell in the uttermost parts of the sea; even there shall thy hand lead me, and thy right hand shall hold me (Psalm 139:7-13)."

This Word became a reality to Jonah when the sailors encountered a fierce, life-threatening storm. And when they ascertained that Jonah was the perpetrator of their condition, they reluctantly threw him overboard. Finally, after Jonah was thrown overboard, a great fish immediately swallowed him and took him on the rollercoaster ride of his life. This deep, dark entombment caused the Prophet Jonah to do some praying and repenting from which God heard him from the belly of Hell (the fish). When the fish finished his deep-sea tour with Jonah, God caused him to spit him out on dry ground.

This prophet of God was so glad to get a second chance that he ran to Nineveh in one day, which was normally a three-day journey. He proclaimed the Word of God to the Ninevehites and the whole city humbled themselves in fasting and praying, and God spared the city. Thank God for waking up the sleeping prophet.

"To obey is better than sacrifice and to hearken than the fat of rams. For rebellion is as the sin of witchcraft, and stubbornness is as iniquity and idolatry. (Samuel 15….22-23)."

CHAPTER VI

SPIRITUAL GIANTS TURNED
THE WORLD UPSIDE DOWN

Part I

Simon Peter felt that he failed God when he denied Jesus three times before his crucifixion. Peter was spiritually weak and unstable like a leaf, but God saw him as a stone and a giant. Peter the giant was spiritually asleep when he denied Jesus. To a certain extent, Peter did not lie when he said he didn't know Jesus as he had not received him in his heart. Of course, that was not Peter's motive at that particular time. But Jesus himself will tell those that never received him in their heart, "I never knew you, depart from me (Matthew 7:23)."

Jesus knew that Peter would be a spiritual rock when he told Peter, "When thou art converted, strengthen you brethren (Luke 22: 32)." God chipped away Peter's exterior until he got to the rock on the inside. Peter always had a zeal for God, but it was only after he was converted and filled with the Holy Spirit that he was able to do supernatural exploits in the name of Jesus, walked on water, healed the sick and he witnessed boldly in spite of extreme opposition.

The other apostles took a bold stand for God and reeked havoc in the Kingdom of darkness. It was said of them "These that have turned the world upside down are come hither also (Acts 17:6)."

The people were afraid of the mighty spiritual powers that was demonstrated by the apostles. Many signs and wonders were wrought among the people by the power of God. "And believers were the more added to the Lord, multitudes of men and women. Insomuch that they brought forth the sick into the streets, and laid them on beds and couches, that at the least the shadow of Peter passing by might overshadow some of them. There came also a multitude out of the cities around about unto Jerusalem, bringing sick folk and them which were vexed with unclean spirits and they were healed every one (Acts 5:14-16)."

This same power will be exhibited by present day Christians when the giant on the inside is awakened by the Holy Spirit of God.

Part II

Acts 12:4-20 gives an account of Peter being incarcerated by order of King Herod for preaching and teaching the Word of God. Herod's plan was to prosecute Peter after the Easter Holiday. But God had other plans for Peter's life. While Peter was in prison, the saints of God had a twenty-four hour prayer vigil going in his behalf. Intercessory prayer warriors are spiritual giants possessing keys to the Kingdom of God. Their faith and prayers are the catalyst that causes reactions in heaven.

On the same night that Herod was to bring Peter forth, God heard their prayers and executed a plan to deliver Peter. He sent an Angel and woke Peter up, who was sleeping between two soldiers. The soldiers did not wake up when Peter got up and his chains and cuffs fell off. Peter dressed himself as the Angel instructed him and followed the Angel out of the prison. Peter thought he was seeing a vision, but he was actually witnessing the power of God in response to prayer.

As Peter followed the Angel through the prison, and up to the big iron gates, which opened up before them on it's own accord, Peter was awakened out of sleep and was set free by the supernatural power of God.

Acts Chapter 10 tells of Peter praying upon the roof when he fell into a trance, seeing heaven open. He saw all kinds of four footed wild beasts, creeping creatures and fowls of the air contained in a great sheet. Peter heard a voice telling him to "Rise, Peter; kill and eat (Acts 10:13)." But Peter answered, "Not so Lord; for I have never eaten any thing that is common or unclean (Acts 10:14)." The voice spoke again saying, "What God has cleansed, that call not thou common (Acts 10:15)." This procedure was done three times, and then was received in heaven. Then Peter was awakened. God showed Peter this vision so that he could see himself, his self-righteousness, his prejudices and feelings of superiority over the people that weren't of Jewish faith.

This story depicts some Christians in the body today who have the same mindset regarding race and religion. These people have to see themselves through revelations and through God's Word the same as Peter. Peter's nap was not a coincident, God allowed him to slumber in order for him to be awaken to the truth. Once Peter saw himself in light of the Word of God, he was not hesitant to go where the Spirit bade him and to do what the Spirit told him to do. Peter testified to Cornelius, "a Gentile 'God has showed me that I should not call any man common or unclean (Acts 10:28)." Than Peter opened his mouth, and said, of a truth I perceived that God is no respecter of person. But in every nation he that

21

.earth him, and worketh righteousness, is accepted with him (Acts 10:34-35)." Jesus Christ is Lord of all.

Part III

Acts chapter 16 gives an account of two more spirituals giants that were used for the glory of God. Paul and Silas were imprisoned, after casting a demon out of a possessed woman. The woman's master made a living from her having the spirit of divination (fortune telling). Once the spirit was gone, so was his money making scheme, which made him furious. Her master brought legal charges against Paul and Silas. The magistrates had them stripped of their clothes, beat them severely and casted them into prison with orders to keep them locked up.

The jailor in response to the strict command of the magistrates placed their hands and feet in stocks and stationed guards around them, making all means of escape impossible. These men were not grieved over their plight or from their physical pain, due to their brutal beatings. They counted it all joy and an honor to be afflicted for the cause of Christ.

Paul and Silas gave vent to their emotions at midnight as they sang praises and prayed unto God. The other prisoners heard them, but most of all God heard them and responded with a great earthquake, which shook the foundation of the prison, opened all the doors and every one that was bound in prison was set free. Praise the Lord!

After this manifestation, God used Paul mightily. Special miracles were wrought by his hands, so much that handkerchiefs and aprons from his body were given to the sick and disease and evil spirits departed from them.

This particular scenario serves as a reminder to the body of Christ to persevere in the faith because when spiritual giants are awakened to the call and cause of Christ, locked doors are opened, captives are released, demons are casted out, strongholds are pulled down, the dead is revived and cities are turned upside down. Souls are saved, the devil is horrified, but God is glorified. Thank God for spiritual giants.

CHAPTER VII

PERSONAL TESTIMONY

En Route to Being Awakened

As I reflect on my past before I became a Christian, my life seem to parallel Abram's life somewhat. God told Abram "Get thee out of thy country, and from thy kindred, and from thy father's house, unto a land that I will shew thee (Genesis 12:1)."

When I questioned God, asking why he brought us to North Carolina from Los Angles, California God spoke the following, "Wherefore come out from among them, and be ye separate, saith the Lord, and touch not the unclean thing; and I will receive you, and will be a father unto you, and ye shall be my sons and daughters, saith the Lord Almighty (2 Corinthians 6:17-18)."

In July 1970, I visited Mount Olive, North Carolina for the first time with my husband Earl, who was a native of Mount Olive. After our visit, Earl became obsessed with moving back home.

I was definitely opposed to his suggestion because I had signed up to go to school to become a Registered nurse. Earl promised me emphatically that if I came to North Carolina he would make sure I had the opportunity to fulfill my lifelong dream as I was already a Practical nurse.

Needless to say, in August 1970, one Tuesday morning we started on a trip to North Carolina that turned into the twilight zone. Neither one of us was saved. We did not have the mind to consult God about anything that was done, we just acted.

Thanks be to God, who knew the plan that he had for our lives, because we sure didn't. We were young, foolish and we made some very bad decisions, but little did we know, God had us on the Potter's wheel.

I had mixed emotions about leaving my four sisters and other family and friends in Los Angeles and going to a place where I had to make a new start. I was not feeling this, at all. Earl, had paid cash for an old Cadillac for our trip, which was the first mistake he made, because it later blew up in the desert. We rented a large U-Haul, which was filled to capacity with our household goods. I drove the car, and Earl drove the U-Haul. Two of my sisters decided to relocate to Atlanta, Georgia. One of my sisters had us to haul her 1965 Mustang with the U-Haul truck and leave it at our parent house in Mississippi until she got there. She sent her two sons with us as well.

As we begin to make our way out of L.A., Earl got a traffic ticket for driving in the inner lane. Then, that old car I was driving blew up in the San Bernardino desert. It started pumping black smoke, leaving a cloud a half mile down the road. There was no shoulder on the road to pull off due to construction and the car was losing pressure while going up an incline on the road. I began to call on God out of sheer desperation. I had no other help and I didn't know what else to do.

My car had backed up traffic for miles on that two-way road. I felt such anguish and fear when the motor blew up. I thought the car would stop in the middle of the road at any moment. I was at the mercy of the Almighty God. No one else could help me. I continued to pray and I began to talk to the car, pleading; "Please don't stop." God heard me and answered my prayer, because the car didn't come to a complete stop, even though it slowed down to 15 miles an hour. Finally, praises be to God! I saw an area where I could pull off on the shoulder of the road and I was so glad, and I'm sure the long trail of people behind me were just as relieved.

It was 120 degrees in the car but we sat there. Finally my husband caught up with us. With no shade in that desert area, Earl pulled the truck in front of the car and he and I and the seven children, crawled under the U-Haul until the sun went down and it began to cool off.

We had to unhook my sister's Mustang for the continuation of our trip, which had not been serviced for the road, nor was it big enough to transport seven children. Earl hooked up the defunct car to the U-Haul and took two of our children with him, I had the other five with me in the Mustang. We were packed like sardines in a can. We got to New Mexico without any problems and went to a picnic area to rest, eat and refresh. I had packed plenty food and drink, because we were not able to buy food due to our limited funds.

I praise God now that Earl had the presence of mind to give me a map, and half of the money in case we got separated because that's exactly what happened. Little did I know I would not see them until Saturday night. After we finished eating in New Mexico, Earl said to the children with him "Come on let's go." He didn't say anything to me. He and the two children got into the U-Haul and drove off. I told my crew to "hurry up, lets clean up and go catch up with Earl." We dumped our trash, jumped in the car, and sped off the way I saw him go.

Well, I drove like a mad woman but I didn't see him. So then, I decided that he was behind me. So I pulled off on the side of the highway, waiting for him to catch up. I waited for hours, but he never came. So I would drive 95 miles an hour thinking he must be in front of me. I played that cat and mouse game with myself until the next day. I began to get tired. I didn't have enough money for a motel, so we would have to sleep in the car. My anxiety level was so high, and I was taking caffeine tablets to stay awake. I tried to make sense out of this craziness.

I arrived in Oklahoma City in rush hour traffic, which was the worst time for me in my current state of mind. I pondered if I should go through that traffic or wait until later. But eventually I decided to go through. It was only by the grace of God, that I was able to maneuver in that traffic to exit the right road at the right time. When I got pass Oklahoma City I was completely exhausted. I had never driven that far alone. Little, did I know that I was not alone. God had Angels watching and guiding me all along the way.

After going through Oklahoma City, I decided I would pull off the road and take a nap. I had resolved in my mind that Earl had gone on to Mississippi and had left me behind. I still couldn't understand why he left me. It was so not like him. He was always protective of me and our children so I had a hard time dealing with being abandoned.

When I finally settled down enough to nap, the children started screaming. I looked in the rear view mirror and saw that someone had pulled up in back of us, two people jumped out of their car and were running towards us, with what looked like a hatchet and a flash light. Before they got to our car, I started the engine, gunned the motor, and sped away. That incident woke me up for a while.

Later I kept falling asleep at the wheel, upon awakening I would feel the terrible, overwhelming feeling of rejection, abandonment, loneliness, and of being shut off from family and friends, and being in a strange land, without a place to call home.

As I continued to drive, I fell asleep at the wheel and was driving 10-15 miles an hour in a construction zone, and was blocking traffic. A big truck came along and pushed me off the road. I stayed awake a long while after that incident. Our oldest daughter, a teenager, stayed awake to make sure I would stay awake while driving.

I was extremely tired, worried, and nervous all at the same time. I was popping pills as well. Then the car started running hot. I didn't know what to do, it was late at night and each service stations I came upon was closed. I drove for miles and finally I saw another service station, which was closed, but I had to get some water, I thought.

I pulled up to the service station and then I looked across the street there was a building with people who had on white sheets (white people) I was so impaired I could not think. I was going to get the water anyway and my daughter said "Mama we had better go from here." So we left, car running hot, very tired, none of us had taken a bath, nor had a decent meal since Tuesday. I was awake for a while thinking about what could have resulted from an encounter with whom I assumed to be Klansmen and it was very late at night. It probably was a good thing that I didn't get to put water in the hot radiator, because I'd probably have gotten burned trying to take the cap off.

The Lord let me drive all night long with the car running hot, and me running off the road. Finally, at 6 am I found a service station open where I got gas and water. The service station attendant couldn't believe that I had driven from Tuesday until Friday alone with those children. I would stop on the roadsides to try to sleep, but the children made so much noise and the heat was so unbearable I could not sleep. Frustrated I drove off again. My nerves got to the point where I felt that I could bend the wheel like an inner tube. I was on the verge of having a nervous breakdown. The wheel was feeling like putty; the soft feeling in my hands was bothersome. The steering wheel was not suppose to feel soft and pliable in my hands like biscuit dough.

Like a zombie, I drove on until I got to Little Rock, Arkansas. My daughter said "Mama why don't you call Grandma in Mississippi and see if daddy's there?" Well the light bulb came on! That never crossed my mind I was so preoccupied with the trip and with driving that I never thought of that. So right away, I found a pay phone, pulled off and called my parent's home, collect, in Mississippi.

My mother was so upset she was crying. She was so glad to hear from me. I asked if Earl was there. She said no, Earl is in New Mexico. She said he has called and called trying to locate you. "Where are you?" She gave me the number where Earl was because he told her he wasn't going anywhere until he heard from me.

I told her I was in Little Rock, Arkansas. She told me to call my sister in California that she was highly upset because Earl had called her looking for us. So I called my sister in L.A. She said, "Dot, where in the world are you? Earl has gone stone crazy. He think you have come back here because he knew you didn't want to go to North Carolina" and she said, "Girl I have put out an APB on you. You are listed as a missing person with all the children (two of them belonged to her)" "Girl call your husband because he has gone stone crazy."

I called Earl from Little Rock, Arkansas right then and he told me our daughter was sick with a fever and he wanted me to stay in Little Rock until he got there from New Mexico. I said "no way." I am going on to Mississippi because I am tired, worn out, and need a bath. Our daughter got well when she knew that I was o.k.

I drove on into Greenwood, Mississippi. When I got there my flesh was quivering, my muscles were twitching, I was haggard and tired to the bone. My father said he had never felt as sorry for anyone as he did for me right at that time. He was in tears, seeing my condition. I took a bath and tried to rest, but I was too tired to relax. I needed a nerve pill but didn't have one. Nor did I or my parents know enough about God to ask him to intervene in my condition.

I finally relaxed enough to sleep a little while, but was awakened about 12 midnight, when Earl driving the U-Haul truck with the other children arrived. We were so glad to see each other. We embraced and shared stories about our saga, which took a very longtime.

On the next day, which was Monday, we left Mississippi to continue our trip to North Carolina. The only obstacle was that we no longer had a car to drive. My sister's Mustang had to be left in Mississippi. That meant that all seven of us had to squeeze into the cab of the U-Haul. Thank God, the children were small. We managed, but it was a tight squeeze.

We arrived in Mt Olive, North Carolina that Tuesday evening. I was ready to go back as soon as we arrived. But I didn't have any money and was to embarrassed and proud to ask my family and friends. So I said I would stay until I got enough money to leave. I was miserable, without having any close family or friends.

I didn't seem to fit in my new environment. My lifestyle was different because I was coming from a different culture. I wore clothing the women in the community frowned upon. I was not a Christian at that time and the only things that they talked about was going to church, which really turned me off. Earl knew I was very unhappy so he introduced me to his former schoolmates, Mr. and Mrs. A.B. She was the first friend that I had. We grew very close and she helped to make my transition smoother. We did many things together, with our families. We would picnic, bowl, and socialize together frequently. I was very grateful for her friendship, which remains until this present day.

The Process of Being Awakened

We moved to Mt Olive during the first year of desegregation, and our children had to endure undue hardship in the school system, which caused a readjustment for them, as well.

Things seemed to get worse, because I couldn't find a job. We had to make do with my husband's limited income at the Mill.

By now, I had learned to pray. One day on my way home, after taking Earl to work, I began to cry out to God, and asked him please, please, give me a job. You see I was so desperate that I was willing to do any kind of work to help make ends meet.

That same day that I prayed, the Employment Security Commission contacted me about a job at Long Term Care Facility in Goldsboro, the neighboring town of Mount Olive. Before coming to North Carolina, I worked at a large hospital. I was very critical and looked down on people who worked in nursing homes. I called them second class professionals, and felt that their skills were inferior to those that worked in a hospital. I voiced

31

my opinion whenever I got a chance. I was full of pride and arrogance. But God humbled me in order to use me. Ironically, the first and only job I could get was in a nursing home, and I was glad to swallow my pride and accept the job.

Remember I still had not been converted. Little did I know that I was on my way. Our children went to Sunday school every Sunday with their cousins at Gospel Light Church. They would come home and share their lesson with me. They would tell me that some children's parent were saved, which aroused my curiosity. Because the term "saved" was not familiar to me in terms of going to church. And in reality, they couldn't explain it.

During my employment at the nursing home, I met some very nice people and some who were not so nice. Even some of the physicians were hostile towards me. But God fought for me. One Christian lady demonstrated her love for God by sharing Christian books with me after she found out that I was not saved. She witnessed to me in a simple loving way. One of the books that she shared with me was the "Rapture." The Second Coming of Christ. This book stirred my very soul. I learned spiritual principles that I never knew before. I also found out that there had been many occasions that I could have died and burned in Hell for all eternity. I didn't put the book down until I finished it.

The Awakening

For the first time in my life, I knew I was lost. I was cooking dinner at that time, I turned the stove off. I was under great conviction, and I did not want to wait another minute. So I went into my bedroom and fell on my knees and I cried out to God. In tears, I confessed my sins and I invited Jesus to come into my heart and save my soul. Oh, praise his name! Immediately, a bright light appeared above my head and the warmth of it swept down over my body and disappeared. I rose up praising God. I could feel the power and presence of the Holy Spirit. I knew for myself what it meant to be saved. Halleluiah!!

I was crying tears of joy as I told my husband that I was saved. He was so concerned, because he had never seen me give vent to the Holy Spirit. He asked me if I was all right, if there was anything he could do for me. I told him that, I had never been so alright in all my life. That all of my sins had been washed away and that my name had been written down in the Book of Life. I was glad to be a new creature in Christ.

I was on fire for God and readily shared my testimony of salvation with all who would listen, especially my family and friends back home. Some of my family members thought I had lost my mind, because of the drastic change in my lifestyle and conversations. My parents were concerned that Earl has taken me to North Carolina where someone had put a spell on me. When they saw me, they looked at me strange, trying to figure out the new person I had become. Little did they know that I was living under the power of the Holy Spirit and that God had changed my whole life. After many years of observing my life, they realized that what I had was real. God used me later on to lead my mother, father, husband, and many other family members to Christ.

Salvation does not exempt anyone from Satan's ploy and tricks. My husband and I made three attempts to go back to California. We were so determined to return back to "Egypt", that we resigned from our jobs and rented a U-Haul to move our belongings. We finally came to the conclusion that it was God's Will for us to stay in North Carolina because all our efforts to leave were absolutely futile. Little did we know that God had a plan for our lives and had brought us here to be processed for his purpose.

After I received Christ as my personal savior, I joined a local church and was baptized for the second time, because I was not saved the first time I was baptized. God awakened in me a hunger and thirst to learn more about his word, and witness to others about his love.

CHAPTER VIII

A DIVINE AWAKENING

I had been fasting and praying for several days, because I wanted a closer relationship with God. On April 4, 1981, at 3:00 am, I was awakened from a deep sleep by three knocks on the front door. I did not get up right away; I began to doze off again when I heard the three knocks a second time. In my spirit, I knew it was not an ordinary knock, nor did I expect to see anyone when I opened the door.

I opened the door and saw no one. While standing at the door looking out, I observed the beauty and felt the peace of God. The moonlight was shimmering on the beautiful multi-colored azaleas in the front yard. I continued to look on in awe and I thought what a great and mighty God!

I had an inclination that the Lord woke me up to pray. So I went to the living room to pray. As I stepped through the doorway, I heard the Lord say, "Ask anything, and I will give it to you." I was so amazed at what I had just heard, that it literally blew my mind. I could not think of money, even though I had a great financial need. I asked three things of the Lord: that my family be saved, to be blessed on my new job at the prison, and for the manifestation of the Holy Spirit.

After making my requests to God, I knelt on a chair to pray. After praying for a while, I was led by the spirit to remain on my knees. The Lord spoke to my heart again, saying, "I am going to bless you exceedingly." "Thank you Lord," I said. The Lord continued to speak to my heart, and after each revelation, I would thank him. The presence of God was awesome as he spoke to me. After communing with God, I remained on my knees, revisiting this captivating experience in my mind.

Suddenly, I saw flickers of lights, which appeared and disappeared right before my very eyes! I was totally captivated as I watched the flicker of lights turn into bright balls of light. The balls grew in dimension and emitted brilliant, dazzling rays of color, like a diamond when it reflects light. I stared in sheer amazement, not believing or understanding what I was seeing. A cluster of lights appeared. It was as if the Lord was leading me into another dimension and doing it in such a way, I would not be scared to death. Even though the lights were very bright, they did not cause me to squint or bat my eyes. I could feel the presence of the Holy Spirit as I continued to look on in awe.

The cluster of lights disappeared, then a white light, larger than all the rest appeared. It was about the size of a small beach ball. It did not flicker, but rose slowly towards the ceiling. My gaze was fixed on this spectacular light, and I rose to my feet as the light ascended. As I was looking directly upward, the most amazing thing happened! The ball of light burst like a balloon, releasing the awesome spirit of God upon me! My body immediately began to tingle. I can only describe that sensation as tiny jolts of electrical current flowing through my body. I felt as if I had stuck my finger into an electrical socket, but I experienced no pain. In response to this holy manifestation, I began to speak fluently in an unfamiliar language. I had been baptized in the Holy Spirit! The Holy Spirit filled and embraced me and I basked in the presence of God.

I praised God for the baptism of the Holy Spirit. When the Spirit allowed me to leave the room, my knees were so weak I could hardly make it back to bed. When I got back into bed, I continued to thank God for his goodness and love shown toward me. The effects of the Holy Spirit were still present in my body. I continued to meditate about what happened. The enemy tried to plant a seed of doubt in my mind saying that I did not see what I thought I saw. The enemy tried to rob me of the joyful experience I had just had with God.

I prayed, "Lord if what I saw was real, give me a sign. Let me see those same lights on the headboard of my bed: immediately, the headboard was lit up with dazzling lights as I had previously seen. I began to smile and praise God. Again, satan said, "Your eyes are fooling you; you did not see what you thought you saw." I was determined that satan was not going to rob me or steal my victory. Again, I prayed, "Dear God, I know what I saw. If that was really You, let me see those same lights upon the wall in a corner beside the bed." Instantly, the wall was aglow with the most brilliant lights that I had ever seen. I was completely convinced beyond a shadow of a doubt that I had a supernatural manifestation from God! I praised the Lord until I fell asleep.

When I woke up the next morning, I felt the need to share my experience with someone who would be excited and rejoice with me. But before I could contact anyone, the Lord spoke to me again and told me to read the word. I said, "Lord, I don't know what to read." I opened the Bible and fastened my eyes upon Isaiah, chapter 42. It read: "Behold my servant whom I uphold… my elect in whom my soul delighteth, I have put my spirits upon him." I continued to read and was refilled with joy. I could not contain myself any longer especially after I read verse seven, which spoke about going into the prison. Remarkably, I had asked God earlier to bless me on my new job, which was in the prison.

I was bursting to tell somebody! I called my friend on her job and told her. We rejoiced together! This open vision has been engraved in my spirit and it serves as a source of comfort and strength in trying times. It also assures me that God loves me and His holy presence will always be with me. I didn't realize at that time that this visitation by God was preparing me to work for Him. Three years later, God begun to speak with me through visions and dreams. Eventually, this lead to my total surrender and acceptance to the call of ministering His word.

"All things that the Father hath are mine, therefore, said I, that he shall take of mine, and shall show it unto you (John 16:15)."

Beloved,
God is real! So real that He will manifest Himself in any form He chooses! He will awaken the sleeping giant to reveal himself in such a personal manner, that you will know without a shadow of a doubt that He is God!

A Prophetic Dream Warning
(To Escape the Coming Storm)

August 14, 1999, I had a dream about a terrible storm. The effects of this storm caused gross flooding and devastation to all living beings. In the dream, I was standing on what seemed to be a hill in the middle of the road. The place where I was standing was dry. But as far as I could see, everything else was submerged under water. The only thing visible was the rooftop of houses. In the dream, I wept sorrowful tears because of the total destruction that surrounded me. The Lord spoke to me and said, "Beware of the coming storm." I woke up abruptly.

I rehearsed this dream in my mind, I knew it meant something because God often shows me visions or dreams before they actually come to pass. Shortly after the dream, my pastor had to go out of town. He asked me to preach. I prayed about what to preach and the Lord allowed me to revisit the dream and His warning-"Beware of the coming storm." It was so profound that I started crying again. Whenever I thought about the dream, it would provoke me to tears. I knew that I had to share this message with the people.

That Sunday, I used this prophetic warning to preach the subject, "Escape the Coming Storm". I shared my dream with the congregation, even though it seemed to have fallen on deaf ears. Nevertheless, I gave the warning. The message was delivered through blinding tears.

September 1999, my dream became a reality. Hurricane Floyd swept in with devastating winds and rain, which caused mass destruction of property, animal, and human lives. Many homes were submerged under water. Some people sought safety in their attics, but still drowned. The media continually gave updated coverage of the mass destruction of the storm. The impact of the storm was worse in some parts of North Carolina than others. The area where we lived did not receive gross flooding. I felt that the dry land on which I was standing in the dream represented our town. We were spared. It was clear to me now why I was weeping. My spirit was grieving because of the impending destruction. God had revealed to me what was to come. It is not God's will that any should perish.

Dear Readers,

Tears are blinding my eyes again as I write. I want to warn you that there is a storm of storms coming. Beware of the coming storm! "And they shall go into the holes of the rock, and into the caves of the earth, for fear of the Lord, and for the glory of his majesty, when he ariseth to shake terribly the earth (Isaiah 2:19)."

"For thus saith the Lord of host, yet once, it is a little while, and I will shake the heavens, and the earth and the sea, and the dry land; and I will shake all nations... (Haggai 2:6-7)." Thanks be to God who has provided us an avenue of escape through Jesus Christ. If you have not invited Jesus into your heart, please yield to his pleading voice. "Behold I stand at the door and knock; if any man hear my voice, and open the door, I will come into him and will sup with him, and he with me (Revelation 3:20)." We that are called by the name of Christ must witness like never before to warn others of the coming storm. We must tell them of the love of God, and the total provision for our lives through the shed blood of Jesus Christ our Lord. May God bless and keep you.

A Dream Warning
(To Awaken the Sleeping Giants)

On August 2, 2011, I dreamed that the rapture was taking place. Upon awakening, I praised God that it was only a dream, had it been a reality, many souls would have been left behind.

In the dream, I was standing outdoors in front of a large dome building. I stared in awe as I begun to see people flying out of the building like birds. I said "Oh my God"!! The rapture is taking place. I saw the smiles on their faces as they were being caught up in midair.

I could feel the awesome presence of the Holy Spirit all around me. It seemed like the people were being drawn by powerful magnets in the sky.

In the dream I was fully cognant of what was happening, and felt a surge of reality, that "this is really it." People were flying at an accelerated pace around me, yet there were many who were walking, seemly unaffected by the people flying over their heads.

I really became concerned, when I realized I was seeing so many people going up, and I remained on the ground. I began to question, why hadn't I been raptured? I knew that I was saved and filled with the Holy Spirit. It was as if I was talking to God because as I pondered this in my mind, the power of God picked me up and I began flying as well. I was so happy as I flew around the lower levels of the sky, but it was short lived because, then the power of God caused me to come down and circle inside the dome building. After that, I flew outside and was back up on my feet on the ground. I was bewildered and disappointed to say the least. The Spirit spoke to me and said "You are going to be caught up, but not now, you have more souls to reach!"

Immediately after that revelation in the dream, I got in a hurry, knowing that I didn't have any time to waste. God had impressed upon my spirit the urgency of the situation. That many souls were at stake.

In the dream, I began to witness to those people that were around me. I began to tell them that Jesus loved them and that He was coming soon for His people. Most of the people I talked to were not interested in what I was saying. There was one woman that I witnessed to who was dressed in a red frilly type dress, she listened to me attentively and asked how she could get saved. I explained the plan of salvation, which she readily accepted. I praised the Lord God for her salvation. I was grateful as I turned my attention to others telling them about Jesus. The Holy Spirit prompted me to look back at the lady that had just gotten saved. When I looked for her, she was not there but her red dress was on the ground,

41

like she had stepped out of it. I asked someone who was standing near her dress, "Where is the woman that had on that dress. The answer was "she is gone."

She got caught up into the sky. I knew within my mind that I had a major role to play in this process. In the dream, I teamed up with a local pastor, and he and I went witnessing to lost souls.

The situation was so urgent, that we felt we didn't have any time to waste, so we split up. He went one way and I went another. We agreed to meet later on. I went to a building nearby and witnessed to lawyers and law enforcing officers, none of which listened to what I was saying to them. At that point, I was awakened from the dream.

I knew that dream was a wakeup call to me, as well as others, to witness like never before. I saw myself in the light of the dream revelation and how I had been complacent in relationship to soul winning.

This dream really got me fired up. I knew that I had to have a plan of action. "He that winneth souls is wise (Proverbs 11:30)." I repented for my slothfulness in the past, prayed for wisdom in winning souls for Christ. After seeking God for divine direction, the Holy Spirit led me to do a prayer walk in my neighborhood, praying as I walked. I knocked on doors and witnessed to all that would listen that one day many souls were saved. Praise the Lord, by then I was on a spiritual high. I sought the Lord for further directions again and the Holy Spirit prompted me to get the local telephone book and begin a prayer call. Many were receptive to my call. Some expressed amazement, especially when the call came at a time of crisis or at a time of a particular need.

Many appeared to be puzzled that prayer was being offered without asking something of them in return. And thus many calls were rejected. In spite of opposition in a three week period, nine souls accepted Christ as their Lord and Savior.

As a result of the prompting of the Holy Spirit flyers were distributed throughout the city. Along with these ministry tools, I was led to initiate a unity prayer for the purpose of bringing local pastors and church leaders of all denominations together to pray, and to strive for church unity and racial reconciliation among the churches. To pray for the cessation of gang violence, drugs, murders in the schools, and many other related problems. I felt that the initiation of change should begin with devout, spirit filled, God fearing leaders of churches. The twenty-four hour prayer wheel is the ministry tool to be used in this unification process. The first unity meeting was initiated on June 28, 2012 at Helping Hands Mission and continues to be held weekly, at Miracles of Faith House of Prayer, Mt Olive, North Carolina.

24 Hour Intercessory Prayer Wheel

THE 24 HOUR PRAYER WHEEL

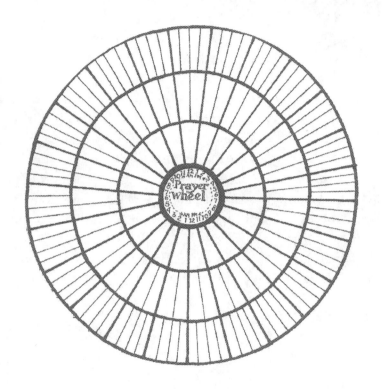

2nd Chronicles 7:14
"If my people who are called by my name will humble
themselves and pray, and seek my face, and turn from
their wicked ways, then will I hear from Heaven,
and will forgive their sin, and will heal their land."

History of the Prayer Wheel

As I was kneeling in prayer on December 1, 1992, praying about the conditions and circumstances in our community; the Holy Spirit moved upon me and inspired me to initiate a systematic way to pray without ceasing. I was obedient to the prompting of the spirit and purchased a poster board and started drawing. While I drew the vision was clear in my mind to draw a (3) three tiered wheel, a wheel in the middle of wheels. I drew as I was inspired by the Holy Spirit. Upon completion of the wheel, I had drawn the three tiers. The first tier represented the 24 hours in a day. The second tier, the 48 one-half hours, and the third wheel represented the 96 one-quarter hours. When the wheel is full, there will be at least seven people praying at all times.

Many hours, day and night was spent making contact with other Christians, soliciting their support and participation on this wheel. Many were eager to pray and was dutiful to pray at the time they committed to. During the time the wheel was initiated, some people in the Mt Olive and Dudley, North Carolina area were experiencing drive by shootings into their homes. Some was shot and some were killed. Many were fearful to sleep in their beds or to stay at home at night. Many slept on the floor. The account of these shootings were on radio, television, and newspapers.

It was only when the twenty-four (24) hour Intercessory Prayer was activated, that the shootings stopped miraculously. Many people wondered why and how these shootings stopped suddenly. A pastor and I was in conversation about these incidents and he voiced in amazement over the cessation of the shootings. I told him I knew it was the Power of Prayer and I shared with him the vision of the prayer wheel.

This Prayer Wheel Ministry has initiated Unity Prayer throughout the Mt Olive and surrounding counties. The prayers continue twenty-four hours daily. Overall bringing Pastors and Community Leaders together that the wall of division be abolished, crossing denominational lines, race and ethnic barriers.

The Prayer Wheel is in circulation in California, Mississippi, Ohio, Pennsylvania and North Carolina. The need for committed and dedicated prayer warriors are still needed to pray on the wheel without ceasing.

The Prayer Wheel Ministry meets every Thursday, at 10:00 AM for Unity Prayer.

THE TIME IS NOW

No one knows the exact time of Christ's return. But we do know that He is coming according to His Holy Word. "But of that day and that hour knoweth no man, no, not thee angels which are in heaven, neither the Son, but the Father (Mark 13:32)"

Now is the time to get right with God. And those that name the name of Christ, should be diligent to fulfill the Will of God for their lives especially as we see the signs of the time unfold. The acceleration of natural disasters, threats of terrorism (which is more greater now than ever), threats of nuclear weapons, moral and spiritual corruption and decay.

The Words of God called to Israel many years ago and the same words speak to us today; "Awake, Awake; put on thy strength, O Zion, put on thy beautiful garments, O Jerusalem, …Shake thyself from the dust; arise… (Isaiah 52:1, 2)."

The Holy Spirit is calling out for Christian giants to wake up and surrender all to the Will of God. If not the Spiritual Giants, then who? If not now, then when?

ABOUT THE AUTHOR

Dorothy Jean Whittaker McDaniel, was born November 2, 1939 in Carroll County, Mississippi. She is the daughter of the late Victoria P. and James E. Whittaker Jr. She is the fifth of nine children.

She was married to the late William E. McDaniel Sr., for 46 years and resides in Mt Olive, North Carolina. Dorothy is a mother, grandmother, and great-grandmother. She is a retired registered nurse.

She is an Evangelist who was called to minister the word in 1986; she is the founder of Miracles of Faith Ministries Inc., Mt Olive, N.C. This ministry encompasses the Twenty-four Hour Intercessory Prayer, and weekly radio ministry.

Dorothy ministers to the disabled, senior homebound and at a senior facility on a regular basis. She is the Recording Secretary for the Interdenominational Ministerial Alliance of Mt Olive. She is an Associate Minister and Elder at Gospel Light United Holy Church of America, Inc. She attended William Carter Christian College and the United Christian College in Goldsboro, NC. Her hobbies include cooking, reading, writing and watching Jeopardy.

She loves to travel and meet new people. Dorothy aspires to reach the pinnacle of God's spiritual assignment through prayer and obedience.

Her Godly wisdom and counsel, as well as her loving nature have made her a valuable asset to the community.